Garfield

Great Impressions

JIM DAVIS

RAVETTE BOOKS

First published by
Ravette Books Limited 1992

Printed and bound in Great Britain
for Ravette Books Limited,
3 Glenside Estate, Star Road, Partridge Green,
Horsham, West Sussex RH13 8RA
An Egmont Company
by Cox & Wyman Ltd, Reading

ISBN 1 85304 191 2

© 1991 United Feature Syndicate, Inc.

© 1991 United Feature Syndicate, Inc.

MAKE MY BIRTHDAY CAKE THIS BIG

JIM DAVIS 6-18

© 1991 United Feature Syndicate, Inc.

© 1991 United Feature Syndicate, Inc.

© 1991 United Feature Syndicate, Inc.

JIM DAVIS 7-6

© 1991 United Feature Syndicate, Inc.

FiSSSS
ZIT ZIT ZIT ZIT
FiSSSS
ZIT ZIT ZIT ZIT

© 1991 United Feature Syndicate, Inc.

© 1991 United Feature Syndicate, Inc.

7-20

JIM DAVIS

© 1991 United Feature Syndicate, Inc.

CLICK-
CHUNK

© 1991 United Feature Syndicate, Inc.

© 1991 United Feature Syndicate, Inc.

JIM DAVIS 7-31

© 1991 United Feature Syndicate, Inc.

© 1991 United Feature Syndicate, Inc

© 1991 United Feature Syndicate, Inc

© 1991 United Feature Syndicate, Inc.

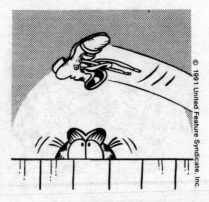

JIM DAVIS 9-5

© 1991 United Feature Syndicate, Inc.

© 1991 United Feature Syndicate, Inc.

© 1991 United Feature Syndicate, Inc.

JIM DAVIS 9-26

© 1991 United Feature Syndicate, Inc.

© 1991 United Feature Syndicate, Inc.

© 1991 United Feature Syndicate, Inc.

JIM DAVIS 10-19

JiM DAViS 10-21

JIM DAVIS 10-25

OTHER GARFIELD BOOKS IN THIS SERIES

GARFIELD GALLERIES

GARFIELD COMIC ALBUMS

COLOUR TV SPECIALS

Here Comes Garfield	£2.95
Garfield On The Town	£2.95
Garfield In The Rough	£2.95
Garfield In Disguise	£2.95
Garfield In Paradise	£2.95
Garfield Goes To Hollywood	£2.95
A Garfield Christmas	£2.95
Garfield's Thanksgiving	£2.95
Garfield's Feline Fantasies	£2.95
Garfield Gets A Life	£2.95
Garfield's Night Before Christmas	£3.95
Garfield's Tales Of Mystery	£3.95
Garfield's Scary Tales	£3.95
Garfield The Easter Bunny?	£3.95
Garfield Best Ever	£4.95
Garfield Selection	£5.95
Garfield His 9 Lives	£5.95
Garfield Diet Book	£4.95
Garfield Exercise Book	£4.95
Garfield Book Of Love	£5.95

All these books are available at your local bookshop or newsagent, or can be ordered direct from the publisher. Just tick the titles you require and fill in the form below. Prices and availability subject to change without notice.

Ravette Books Limited, 3 Glenside Estate, Star Road, Partridge Green, Horsham, West Sussex RH13 8RA.

Please send a cheque or postal order and allow the following for postage and packing. UK: Pocket-books—45p for one book, 20p for a second book and 15p for each additional book. TV Specials —45p for one book plus 30p for each additional book. Other titles—85p for one book plus 50p for each additional book ordered.

Name ....

Address ....

....